Celebrations
NEW YEAR

Jane Cooper

Celebrations

Christmas
Easter
Hallowe'en
Harvest

Hindu Festivals
Jewish Festivals
Muslim Festivals
New Year

All words that appear in **bold** are
explained in the glossary on page 46

First published in 1989 by
Wayland (Publishers) Limited
61 Western Road, Hove
East Sussex BN3 1JD, England

© Copyright 1989 Wayland (Publishers) Limited

British Library Cataloguing in Publication Data
Cooper, Jane
    New year.
    1. New year festivals
    I. Title   II. Series
    394.2'683

ISBN 1 85210 823 1

Phototypeset by Kalligraphics Limited, Horley, Surrey
Printed and bound in Italy by G. Canale & C.S.p.A., Turin

Contents

New Year around the world

Everybody celebrates New Year. However, not all countries celebrate New Year at the same time. This is because people in different parts of the world use different **calendars**.

Each country has its own way of celebrating New Year. These people are from Nigeria, in Africa. They are taking part in a dance at a New Year festival.

People have always been interested in time. Long ago, they divided time into days, months and years. They wrote down their plan of the months of the year in a calendar.

Some calendars are based on the movement of the moon. Some are based on the position of the sun in the sky. Others are based on the positions of the sun *and* the moon.

All over the world, there are special beliefs about New Year. In Hong Kong, for example, peach blossom is said to bring good luck at the time of New Year.

New Year festivals long ago

Ancient Egypt

The Egyptians made a very accurate calendar about 3,000 years ago. Every year the River Nile flooded. Just before it did so, they saw that the star called Sirius appeared in the sky. They measured their year from one appearance of Sirius to another. This gave a year of just over 365 days. It takes 365 days for the earth to travel round the sun.

◀ The Egyptians honoured their god Amon at New Year. He is shown in this painting as the sun.

We know a great deal about the Egyptians because many of their paintings, like this one, have survived on the walls of **tombs**.

The Egyptians began their New Year at the time the River Nile flooded, near the end of September. The flooding of the Nile was very important. Without it, the people would not have been able to grow crops in the dry desert.

At New Year, statues of the god Amon and his wife and son were taken up the Nile by boat. For a month there was singing, dancing and feasting. Then the statues were taken back to the temple.

Babylonia

Babylonia was an important kingdom at about the same time as Ancient Egypt. It lay in what is now the country of Iraq.

The Babylonians made a calendar about 4,000 years ago. It was based on movements of the sun and moon. Their calendar had twelve months, each with thirty days in it. This made a year of 360 days. This is shorter than a full year of 365 days, so an extra month had to be added sometimes to make up the difference.

◀ This is the Babylonian calendar, written on stone.

The Babylonian New Year was in spring. During the festival the king was stripped of his clothes and sent away. For a few days everyone could do just what they liked. Then the king returned in a grand procession, dressed in fine robes. Everyone had to go back to work and behave properly. So, each New Year, the people made a new start to their lives.

This is a carving of a Babylonian king and queen at a feast in a garden.

◀ The Roman god Janus had two faces. One looked back to the past and one looked forward to the future.

The Romans

For a long time the Romans celebrated New Year on the first day of March. Then, in 46 BC, the Emperor Julius Caesar began a new calendar. This was more accurate. It divided the year into the twelve months that we still use today.

The new calendar changed the date of the New Year. It now became the first day of January.

January is named after the Roman god Janus, who was always shown as having two heads. He looked back to the last year and forward to the new one.

The Roman New Year festival was called the *Calends*. Everyone enjoyed themselves. They decorated their homes and gave each other gifts. For a few days, people could do what they liked.

◀ The Romans enjoyed themselves at New Year. Slaves and their masters ate and drank together.

The Celts

The Celts were the people who lived in Gaul (now France) and parts of Britain before the Romans arrived there. The Celts had a special New Year festival called *Samhain*. This word means 'summer's end'. It took place at the end of October.

◀ At *Samhain*, Celts gathered **mistletoe** to keep ghosts away.

Samhain was a rather gloomy festival. The Celts believed this was the time when ghosts of dead people returned to haunt the living. Celtic priests, called druids, went into the forest to collect mistletoe. This was supposed to keep ghosts away.

Some of these ideas are remembered today. At Hallowe'en time in Europe, people still think of ghosts. Hallowe'en takes place at the end of October – the same time of year as *Samhain*.

A Samhain cake is fun to make. It is an old kind of fortune-telling.
Make up a cake mix and add these objects: a ring (for marriage); a coin (for wealth); a button (for an unmarried life); a piece of rag (for poverty). Bake the cake, then share it with friends. See who gets each of the objects.

Jewish New Year

The Jewish calendar goes back about 3,500 years, to the time of **Moses**. Moses divided the year into fifty-two weeks. Each week had seven days.

◀ Moses led the Jewish people out of slavery in Egypt.

This picture shows the Jews leaving Egypt.

Moses made the seventh day of each week a holy
day. This is called the Sabbath. Jews celebrate the
Sabbath each Saturday. Moses also decided that
New Year should be at the beginning of autumn.

The Jewish New Year is called *Rosh Hashanah*. It is
a holy time when people think of the things they
have done wrong in the past. They promise to do
better in the future.

Special services are held at *Rosh Hashanah*. At these services an instrument called a *Shofar* is played. It is made from a ram's horn. The man in this picture is blowing a *Shofar*.

There are celebrations at New Year, too. Children are given new clothes and families eat a special dinner together. New Year loaves are baked and fruit is eaten to remind people of harvest time.

During New Year, Jewish people everywhere attend special services in the **synagogue**. They promise to make a new start and lead better lives.

Muslim New Year

Muslims follow the religion called Islam.

Muslim holy buildings are called **mosques**. This mosque is in Egypt. The very tall thin tower is called a minaret.

The Muslim calendar is based on the movements of the moon. This makes the Muslim year shorter than 365 days. So the date of New Year is eleven days earlier each year.

These Muslims in India are celebrating New Year with a procession.

19

Iran is a Muslim country. It used to be called Persia. In Iran there are some special New Year celebrations. These are older than the religion of Islam. New Year in Iran is always celebrated on the same day each year – 21 March.

A few weeks before this, people put grains of wheat or barley in a little dish to grow. By the time of New Year, the grains have produced shoots. This reminds people of spring and a new year of life.

Some Iranians light fires at New Year and jump over them. They hope this will give them good luck. In ancient times, Persians worshipped fire. Their god was Ahura Mazda. He is shown in this picture, which is 2,000 years old.

Hindu New Year

Most Hindus live in India. Not all Hindus in India celebrate New Year in the same way and at the same time.

The people of West Bengal, in northern India, like to wear flowers at New Year, especially pink, red, purple or white flowers. Women like to wear yellow, which is the colour of spring. This woman is making flower decorations.

In Kerala, in southern India, mothers put food, flowers and little gifts on a special tray. On New Year's morning, children have to keep their eyes closed until they have been led to the tray.

21

This is *Lakshmi*, the Hindu goddess of wealth.

People all over the world look to the future at New Year. They hope to be happy, healthy and successful. At New Year, Hindus think particularly of the goddess of wealth.

In central India, orange flags are flown from buildings on New Year's Day.

In Gujarat in western India, New Year is celebrated at the end of October. It takes place at the same time as the important Indian festival of *Diwali*.

◀ This old picture shows an Indian prince celebrating *Diwali*. Fireworks are being set off in the background.

At the festival of *Diwali*, Indian families make little oil lamps and burn them like this. They can look beautiful in the darkness.

The word *Diwali* means 'cluster of lights'. At the time of this festival, small oil lights are lit all along the roofs of buildings. *Diwali* takes place all over India. In Gujarat the lights are also a sign of the beginning of a new year.

New Year in the Far East

In some countries in the Far East many people are **Buddhists**. These Buddhist girls in Burma are throwing coloured water over each other at New Year.

At the time of New Year, people in these countries like to wash their statues of the Buddha with scented water.

People also throw water over each other at New Year festivals. They hope this will bring them a good rainy season. Then they will have good crops.

One Far Eastern New Year custom is to let pet animals go free. Sometimes people buy a turtle in a market at New Year. They decorate its shell with gold paper. Then they let it go. People believe being kind to animals will bring them good luck in the year to come.

You can make scented water for yourself. Soak flowers, leaves, herbs or spices in very hot water. Try using lavender, rose petals, cloves or nutmeg.

These men live on Sumba, an island in Indonesia. At New Year they fight each other on horseback. They believe some bloodshed will make their crops grow better. The spears are blunt so nobody is hurt.

The Chinese calendar is about 3,500 years old. Its months are measured by the movement of the moon. The year is measured by the sun. This means an extra month has to be added from time to time. New Year is celebrated some time between 17 January and 19 February, at the time of the new moon.

Animal years

Rat—1960, 1972, 1984

People born in the daytime will have an easy life. Those born at night will work hard.

Ox—1961, 1973, 1985

Patient, thoughtful and a hard worker.

Tiger—1962, 1974, 1986

Faithful to friends.

Rabbit—1963, 1975, 1987

Happy and contented.

Dragon—1964, 1976, 1988

Likes to be alone.

Snake—1965, 1977, 1989

Clever, good at doing things.

Chinese people give each year the name of an animal. They say that we are like the animal whose year it was when we were born. The chart on these two pages shows you the animals of the Chinese calendar. Can you work out which animal you are? Remember that the year starts in late January or early February.

Horse—1966, 1978, 1990

Strong and friendly.

Ram—1967, 1979, 1991

Proud, but good at helping other people.

Monkey—1968, 1980, 1992

Very curious, learns quickly.

Cock—1969, 1981, 1993

Proud and works hard.

Dog—1970, 1982, 1994

Faithful to friends and quick to learn.

Pig—1971, 1983, 1995

Intelligent, but easily upset.

There is a story behind these animals and their years. Long ago, the animals decided to race across a river to decide whose year should come first. The ox was the best swimmer. But the rat cleverly jumped on the ox's back as he swam and then jumped off at the last moment. So he reached the river bank first. That is why the Year of the Rat comes first.

Chinese New Year is called *Yuan Tan*. It is celebrated by Chinese people all over the world. This is a Chinese New Year parade in Australia.

The Chinese people believe there are evil spirits around at New Year. So they let off firecrackers to frighten the spirits away. Sometimes they seal their windows and doors with paper to keep the evil spirits out.

Street processions are an exciting part of the Chinese New Year. Every procession includes a dragon. It has a long body which is moved by people inside the costume.

This is a Lion Dance in Hong Kong, performed by people dressed up as a lion and a dragon.

The Vietnamese celebrate the same New Year as the Chinese. They call it the *Tet* festival. Chinese and Vietnamese people believe that there is a god in every home. At the time of New Year, this god travels to heaven. There he will say how good or bad each member of the family has been in the past year.

The Vietnamese used to believe that the god travels on the back of a fish called a carp. Sometimes they buy a live carp at New Year. Then they let the fish go free in a river or pond.

◀ This is a carp. It looks quite like a goldfish.

The Chinese and Vietnamese make paper money and burn it at New Year as an offering to their **ancestors**.

The Vietnamese also believe that the first person to enter their house at New Year will bring either good or bad luck. They try to make sure it will be someone who will bring good luck!

In Japan, people now celebrate New Year on 1 January, as in Europe and the USA. But they also keep some beliefs from their religion, which is called **Shinto**. To keep out evil spirits they hang a rope of straw across the front of their houses.

Some people wear Japanese dress at New Year. The woman in red is wearing a **kimono**. She is praying at a holy place.

Long ago, some people called the Hmong lived in southern China. Now they live all over the Far East.

The Hmong have beliefs about evil spirits at New Year. They clean up the whole house and get all the dust, dirt and soot together. They take it outside and put it near a rope that has been tied to a tree in a loop. Then they jump in and out of the rope loop. The spirits in the dirt try to follow, but they get confused and go away. In this way the Hmong people get rid of evil and bad luck at each New Year.

This is a Hmong New Year game. Two rows of children face each other. They throw a large, soft ball between them. If anybody lets the ball drop they have to pay a **forfeit**.

New Year in the West

Long ago, the Roman Emperor Julius Caesar made 1 January the first day of the year. We still celebrate New Year on this date.

Processions are part of New Year all over the world. This is a New Year festival in California, USA.

This is a New Year's Day football game in California.

When European sailors began to explore the world they took their calendar with them, to North and South America, Africa and the Far East. It is used in the USA, Australia and New Zealand.

The first day of January is now accepted as New Year's Day almost everywhere. Of course, Hindus, Chinese, Jews, Muslims and others still have their own New Years as well.

In Europe, New Year was often a time for **superstition** and fortune-telling.

German girls used to try to find out who they would marry. They dropped hot metal into water and hoped it would form the first letter of their future husband's name.

Girls in Ireland used to put ivy, mistletoe or holly underneath their pillows at New Year. They hoped it would make them dream about the man they would marry.

In England, girls dropped egg white into water. They thought it would form the first letter of the name of the man they would marry.

In Greece, girls used to eat something salty before going to bed. They believed this would help them to dream about their future husband.

This person has made a fantastic face from moss, leaves and nuts. It is worn on Saint Sylvester's Eve.

In some parts of Switzerland and Austria, people dress up to celebrate Saint Sylvester's Eve on New Year's Eve.

In AD 314 there was a **Pope** called Saint Sylvester. People believed that he captured a terrible sea monster. They thought that, in the year 1000, this sea monster would escape and destroy the world. As the year 1000 came, everyone was terrified. But the New Year passed without any disaster. Everyone was delighted!

Since then, in parts of Austria and Switzerland, this story has been remembered at the time of New Year. People dress up in fantastic costumes. They are called *Sylvesterklauses*.

◀ *Sylvester-klauses* wear huge bells and very strange hats!

In Greece, New Year's Day is also the Festival of Saint Basil. He helped start the Greek Church.

Saint Basil was famous for his kindness. Greek children leave their shoes by the fire on New Year's Day. They hope he will come and fill the shoes with presents.

Greek people bake a New Year cake with a ring in it.
A piece is sometimes given to the family's donkey.

The cake comes from a story about Saint Basil,
telling how he helped poor people to pay their taxes.
He took some jewellery from each person and gave it
to the Governor. The Governor was sorry for the
poor people, and gave the jewellery back. But Basil
did not know who owned each piece of jewellery.
Then a **miracle** happened. He baked each piece
inside a loaf and when the loaves were given out,
everyone got the right jewellery back!

In Scotland, New Year is a special time. The Scottish call it Hogmanay.

In some Scottish villages at Hogmanay barrels of tar are set alight and rolled through the streets. In this way the old year is burned up and the new one allowed in.

Scottish people honour the poet Robert Burns just after New Year. It is the custom on Burns' Night for a piper to play as a **haggis** is brought to the table.

One important part of Hogmanay. is called first-footing.

Scottish people believe that the first person to enter your house in the New Year will bring good or bad luck. It is very good luck if the visitor is a dark-haired man bringing a gift. This custom is called first-footing.

Scottish people sing a song called *Auld Lang Syne* at midnight on New Year's Eve. They hold hands in a circle and wish their friends luck for the next year. This custom is now celebrated all over the world.

Glossary

Ancestors Members of your family who lived long ago.

Buddhists Followers of the religious teacher called the Buddha.

Calendar A system for dividing the year into different months.

Forfeit A penalty you pay when you make a mistake or lose in a game.

Haggis A Scottish pudding made from meat and oatmeal and cooked in a sheep's stomach.

Kimono A Japanese robe that is wrapped around you and ties at the waist.

Miracle An amazing event which people believe was caused by God.

Mistletoe An evergreen plant with white berries which grows on trees. It is often used as a Christmas decoration.

Moses The leader of the Jews long ago. He led them out of Egypt to freedom.

Mosque A holy building where Muslims meet to pray.

Pope The leader of the Roman Catholic church.

Shinto The main religion in Japan.

Superstition Belief in the supernatural.

Synagogue A holy building where Jews meet to pray.

Tomb A place where the dead are buried.

Books to read

These books will tell you
more about New Year.

Chinese New Year by Anne
    Bancroft (Macdonald,
    1984)
Customs and Ceremonies by
    Elizabeth Holt and Molly
    Perham (Evans Brothers,
    1980)
Festivals by Beverley Birch
    (Macdonald, 1984)
Highdays and Holidays by
    Margaret Joy (Faber &
    Faber, 1981)

Acknowledgements

The publisher would like to thank all those who provided pictures on the following pages: Australian Information Service, London 30; British Tourist Authority 45; Camerapix Hutchison Library 4, 5, 24, 25, 27, 33; Camera Press 16; Bruce Coleman (M. Freeman) 19, (Hans Reinhard) 32; Bill Donohoe 13, 26, 35, 39, 43; Mary Evans Picture Library 14, 38, 42; Hong Kong Tourist Association 31; Hutchison Library cover; The Mansell Collection 11, 15; Wendy Meadway 28, 29; Ann & Bury Peerless 22, 23; Peter Newark's Western Americana 12; Outlook Films Ltd. 7, 18; PHOTRI 17, 36; Rex Features Ltd. 37, 40, 41; Scottish Tourist Board 44; Ronald Sheridan's Photo-Library 6, 8, 9, 10, 20; TOPHAM 34; Wayland Picture Library 21.

Index